Saying
Goodbye

Saying
Goodbye

PATRICIA A. SAUNDERS

Archway Publishing books may be ordered through booksellers or by contacting:

Archway Publishing
1663 Liberty Drive
Bloomington, IN 47403
www.archwaypublishing.com
844-669-3957

Interior Image Credit: Patricia A. Saunders
Author's photo credit: LaLa Photography

ISBN: 978-1-6657-4826-1 (sc)
ISBN: 978-1-6657-4827-8 (e)

Library of Congress Control Number: 2023915093

Print information available on the last page.

Archway Publishing rev. date: 09/07/2023

Table of Contents

"Finally, brethren, farewell. Be perfect, be of good comfort, be of one mind, live in peace, and the God of love and peace shall be with you." - 2 Corinthians 13:11

Acknowledgment

This book is dedicated to my late sister Barbara Williams who was a trailblazer in her time. She traveled the world and was dedicated to the youth. She also wrote poetry and was named "Akousa" on a trip to Ghana. In her final year, as she reflected on her life and shared stories, we had so much in common. She said she lived a good life, knew she was loved, and felt all the prayers. She fought a good fight, with so many words to say, the hardest being "Saying Goodbye."

Also, I acknowledge my late parents, mother, Rev. Betty L. Saunders and my father, Oscar A. Saunders, Sr., who shared with me, "Have the faith of a mustard seed," know that you are unique, and they loved me unconditionally.

To my remaining siblings, nieces, and nephews, "I love you a bushel and a peck and a hug around the neck."

To my supporters, I appreciate meeting you, the reviews, and the feedback to take to heart. You have made me a better writer. Especially my beta readers Miles Warren and Joelle Duarte-Damewood for their time, dedication and honest feedback.

Lastly to my editor, Paulette Nunlee, for being patient with me during my tears, her dedication during a severe thunderstorm with no power to see this book come to fruition.

The Eldest and Youngest

The bond with a sister can't be broken. They are your first advisor, best friend, and protector. Webster's dictionary defines a *sister* as "a female with one or both parents in common with another individual."[1] Being the youngest of a blended family of thirteen, I had six sisters and six brothers. My sisters were there to babysit me while my mother worked in the factory or cleaned houses. They bragged years later that they bought my clothes, changed my diapers, and spanked me when I misbehaved. At school I also bragged about my siblings. Receiving twelve dolls for Christmas and being an aunt at an early age. My father's children were already married when I was born.

My mother had five children from her first marriage. The oldest was Barbara, a beautiful chocolate sister. She became the second mother at thirteen when my mother divorced, responsible for handling the household. Growing up in a small town, she aspired to be more than a housewife, teacher, or secretary. She left for North Carolina to study accounting at a Historically Black College University, and my mother would send money to help with her books. In her first year, she received a call from my mother. She was pregnant and wouldn't be able to continue sending money to her first born. It was time to make changes.

Barbara was different. She set the bar for the rest of her siblings.

---

[1]

Slowly, we each followed in her footsteps. Education was our way out of this small town in Waterbury, Connecticut. Although we went different paths, we had to get our education. An early memory was a newspaper article showcasing my sisters who were all getting associate, bachelor, and master's degrees simultaneously. Barbara had gotten her Master's and was working for large accounting firms. She lived in New York, Washington, D.C., and was moving to Los Angeles. I looked forward to her return visits, listening to grown folks' conversations around the kitchen table and Mom making her favorite deep-dish apple pie. She was making large sums of money, having adventures traveling, and I wanted to be her. I remember, as a teenager, writing a poem about each of my sisters, describing each attribute that I could see from a youth perspective. She was my idol. She made it out: educated and successful.

When I turned eighteen, my graduation gift was to fly solo to California to visit my beautiful sister who was living in the Oakland Hills. Barbara was getting her hair done at the same place as Camille Cosby, spending five hundred dollars on lingerie, and drinking Rémy Martin. She treated me like a mini-princess and exposed me to a life I would later lust to be a part of. She dropped me off at a hair salon where she did their bookkeeping. I got my hair done like Farrah Fawcett. She picked me up, and we drove to Sausalito, with the wind blowing in my hair, for Chicago-style pizza. I felt like a movie star being in California and not having my hair packed in blue Ultra Sheen grease. The California sun kissing my face made me love the space I shared with her.

Though Barbara was nineteen years older, I didn't have the same type of relationship with her that I had with the other siblings. There weren't phone calls except occasionally for advice; I knew if I needed her, she was available. But there was a distance.

In 1993, I returned to California for my niece's high school graduation. I told Barbara I wanted to move to California. My father had explained I needed to become independent and shared that his health was declining. Helping me to develop a plan, she spoke to her boss at a local newspaper about a job for her little sister. I nailed the interview and left with a job. When I returned as an account executive, I would live with her but be responsible for my expenses.

The rule was that on the weekends, I had to leave her house. In August, I came to California on a one-way ticket with two suitcases and my Volvo being delivered later.

The reality came within weeks that I needed to find another residence to have a place I could call home. And not have to roam the Oakland streets until it was clear to come home. I was on the grind to survive and had an apartment and a new job shortly afterward. Within four years, I was meeting new friends and spending holidays with family and friends. I was happy until I received the call my father had passed.

In 1998, I had a new job at the telephone company. I purchased my first home in Antioch, a bedroom community over an hour from my family. I had Barbara come to ensure the documents were in order before I signed on the dotted line. I was excited to have this home built from the ground up until I realized when health scares happened, I was alone.

It was 2002; I met Barbara for lunch at LeChevel, a Vietnamese restaurant she had introduced me to years earlier. Since I had gotten laid off, I thought I needed to be closer to my family. Again the *advisor* asked me questions to test if I was serious. I told her I had it planned when I got a new job I would then move. She said, "Move now while you are not working,". That nudge lit a fire under me. I came home and found a flyer from a realtor on my door. I called her, and within a month, I was packing. The home had sold, and I was back in Hayward.

Our relationship blossomed with more calls, birthday cards, and sharing our love for poetry. I was attending her poetry readings at La Pena Cultural Center in Berkeley, where she had a congo player and a male friend reciting his response to her poetry. She had registered for poetry writing courses and had her works published along with fellow creative minds in the class.

There were daily calls on my way to work telling all the details of my hostile work environment, and her sharing from her past experiences what I might do. I was sharing about falling in love with the wrong men, the sex with them. Reminiscing about the best sex, I realized we had so much in common. No children, homeowners, men, affairs that are not to share beyond the pages. Later going through photos sharing trips to the Bahamas at different phases in our lives, both meeting Will Downey and poetry. We were both powers-of-attorney for my late mother.

It was 2004 when my mother visited and we noticed something was wrong. Barbara orchestrated her return trip and sent my sister to accompany my mother to her doctors. Our world turned upside down. Surgeries and taking turns staying in the hospital in Waterbury for two months.

Our queen would come to California to live, and I would be a power of attorney. Barbara would be my mentor and assist me in making decisions beyond my scope. Our bond deepened during this period because I was responsible for my mother; my siblings had eyes on me. There were times she pulled back, feelings were hurt, and I moved accordingly.

December 30, 2006, at 7:30 am, my mother took her last breath, and I died with her. No one realized it but Barbara. Everyone went to their places, and she realized I was alone with no one to console me. She invited me to spend the night at her home and we had New Year's Eve dinner with her fiancé at the Fat Lady Restaurant in Oakland. I ate like I hadn't in a year; she joked about it. Months later I was in over my head. The depression was more than I could handle; I was giving up on life. Not working, not paying bills, creditors closing in. There was resentment hovering over the relationships with my siblings because I had no place to go and they had no room for me to stay.

I had a family heirloom I'd inherited when my mother passed, and the person in possession refused to relinquish it before their death. The family was divided over the distribution of my mother's personal belongings. I told my siblings about my financial situation, that I needed help. Barbara—the big sister and advisor—shared what I needed to do. Another secret she revealed to me about a common situation. I was selling the second home and its furniture now. So much sentimental meaning because my late mother had blessed it. Still no job yet and needing another place to live. Barbara's words: "You can live at a shelter," cut through me like a knife. No place to go. No money. Account overdrawn. And I put the mask on like I was good.

God had my back; I found an apartment in 2007 with no money, a contract from the pending sell of my house, and an offer letter for a new job.

In 2008, flames in the apartment spread like wildfire in the building. I had to move again, and family and friends came to pack me up. Barbara arrived and didn't say anything until after I moved into the new apartment. She didn't know how depressed I was until she saw I lived in a dark apartment where the sun didn't shine.

During this time, I wrote out my goals; Barbara was supportive. I let her know I would obtain my Master's, purchase another home, and pursue writing a book. I enrolled in 2009 in the online program with the University of Phoenix to get a Master's degree, to the disbelief of others who laughed when I told them. I purchased the third home in 2010, and she suggested an intimate housewarming, small compared to the massive one in 2003 when I had purchased my second home. When I walked across the stage in 2011, she was sitting there cheering me on and letting me know how proud she was of me. In 2012, I wrote *Through the Fire*, and she was there at the book signing. She later let me know—in an argument—her disappointment while sharing events that happened before I was born.

Health scares kept creeping into our lives. Barbara was diagnosed with lung cancer. Seeing her drugged up, tubes in her petite body, I was scared I'd lose her. I had fibroids removed every four years until my fate of never being able to have kids. It was 2013. I had rotator cuff surgery, and my two sisters cared for me. I spent a week at Barbara's; this was the first time since I was a kid she had to bathe me. Selfless and being in the shower with me, we laughed, and I cried. There were many conversations shared that week, and I confessed a desire to pledge to a sorority and the reason. Big sister supported me when I didn't get chosen. While in Washington, D.C., in 2014, she emailed me a photo of the sorority headquarters. Though she never pledged, she shared the desire instilled in us never to give up. "If you can see it, you can achieve it."

Barbara accomplished a lot in her life. She was a founding member of the National Black Accountant Association, a controller for major accounting firms, and diverse careers. Not a quitter, she worked part-time to being a tenured professor at a local community college. Service on the board of directors for non-profits, chairperson for the business departments, and mentor to several in the community. She created an entrepreneurs course for startups needing more tools to sustain themselves. Finding love in her sixties, she married, telling others you could find love if you open your heart and throw out the wish lists of what you're looking for. Still writing poetry, drawing, and painting classes, she was expressing herself. She prepared to retire, writing her goals to achieve it.

I had shared my poetry with my big sister, my work experiences, and my relationship. She was always giving advice, sometimes tough love, but understanding she had already been there and could have written her book about it. She avoided taking on her siblings' burdens but didn't let anyone mess with her family. She would talk to each of us on the phone. She reminded me of my mother in regards to my sister knowing all of our stories and sharing them with the others. That let them know we needed to talk to our brother or sister because she knew that they had gone through something similar but hadn't shared.

The eldest, a Libra, an elegant personality, stubborn, and host of the parties, she had to have checks and balances. You could come to her with an idea, and she would say, "I know you didn't ask for my advice... but." Then she would say she thought about it and did her research, and here are her thoughts. The youngest, there was a stigma that I was irresponsible. Some jobs were challenging, and treatment unfair, and I quickly said, "I'm going to quit." Barbara reassured me,

"You're young. You can find another job and return to where you were. Don't worry about it."

During a visit from my sister and brother-in-law, he shared that he wanted to relocate to Charlotte, North Carolina, before retiring. He shared all the benefits he had researched, and I listened.

It was in 2019 that I felt the desire to relocate and find something new. There wasn't anything holding me in California. I wasn't in a relationship, my job wasn't satisfying, and the equity was outstanding in my house. I shared my thoughts with my sister who discouraged the move.

In 2020, the world shut down to Covid, and my family—as close as we were—didn't go without being touched by the disease. Family members who were already ill required taking precautions to be around. Barbara, a lung cancer survivor, being one of them. We were used to spending the holidays together, and being forced to isolate in our homes was different. We learned how to use technology to see each other. Texting and talking more than usual. We were looking out for each other on places to go for testing, then obtain the shots and booster shots. Again being the protective one in the family, if one got Covid, I was sending care packages from Costco. I feared I didn't want to lose my siblings. They were all I had left.

In 2021, I still had the desire that another place was calling my name and was declaring again my desire to move to North Carolina. So I planned a lunch date with my siblings. I drove and picked up each one from their residence, and we laughed and reminisced over barbecue. Then I told them I wanted to move to North Carolina and would begin visiting to familiarize myself with the state and cities. They had objections, but I let them know there would be a room for them to visit and that they were older, married, and had lived their lives. I needed to move to find the love I desired. Soon after that day, Barbara called and the promise was made.

Longevity ran in my family. Mom was eighty years old when she passed, and Barbara hadn't turned seventy-five. "Don't move yet!" I agreed putting my decision on pause.

Be Careful of
What You Fear

Being a child of older parents, my father sixty, and my mother thirty-nine; my childhood differed. I was used to receiving social security at five years old, people thinking my father was my grandfather, and knowing there were limitations to what I would have compared to others. I loved my parents, but I knew from seeing other kids, their parents were much younger. Whatever they couldn't provide, my siblings stepped in.

I knew about wills and separations before I turned fifteen. I wanted my parents to live forever, and recall the day my parents drove to my West Haven, Connecticut, apartment to let me know my dad had prostate cancer. At twenty-three, that reality was going to hit. Losing someone I love and wanting to hold on to them and not let go was my unrealistic mindset.

On my father's side of the family, I had four brothers, two sisters, and a nephew who succumbed to cancer. I lost my Uncle Jack to cancer. It is the scarlet letter hanging over my family.

On my mother's side, it claimed two cousins. The majority had diabetes and high blood pressure, so it meant strokes and heart disease. They died from complications of a stroke, so whatever was the highest risk was attacking my family on both sides.

"About 224,080 new cancer cases and 73,680 cancer deaths occurred among Black people in 2022. Black people have the highest death rate and shortest survival of any racial/ethnic group in the United States for most cancers."[2]

I have been tested numerous times for breast, tongue, and uterine cancers; all tests were negative. God is good, but the fear still resides in my mind. I have high blood pressure, and am pre-diabetic. So, the fear was confirmed.

Studies show blacks have the highest risk of cancer, making you wonder about the locations where we live, the food we eat, or what we are exposed to.

My sister used to smoke cigarettes and had stopped over twenty years prior. What made her persist in getting tested was my mother never smoked but had been diagnosed with lung disease we were never told she had. The doctors took a good part of my sister's lung; she had to take physical therapy to learn how to function and had inhalers because she also had emphysema. She was tested every year to assure it didn't come back. She and the family shared that she was in remission and going on nine years cancer-free.

I wrote a poem called "Looking Over My Shoulder" about the frustration my sister was experiencing about having to be tested, feeling that she had it cut out, it was gone forever. Tired of being tested, she was faithful in keeping her appointments. She even joked about being the oldest who was the healthiest.

In my research, I Googled to find ways to prevent cancer, and she followed all the tips.

1. If you smoke, stop
2. Eat a lot of fruits and vegetables. Limit meat consumption
3. Exercise
4. Protect yourself from the sun
5. Maintain a healthy weight

2

6. She was vaccinated and had the booster
7. Stay on top of your medical care

It's so strange that cancer will sneak up in the strangest places and attack those I love. I have seen people, young and old, who I've known for years and then their families will share a post on social media they lost the battle.

When an individual discovers they have cancer, it impacts their village. Their *village* is defined as friends, family, and coworkers. They provide support beginning the moment they find a symptom, tell someone, make an appointment with the doctor, get a referral, have a biopsy, and receive the results. You're riding the emotional rollercoaster with them.

In 2012 when we were told Barbara had lung cancer, it was the calmness in her voice that assured her village it was caught early, and she was going to be okay. Having the best doctors, she didn't worry. She celebrated her birthday in the hospital, and I'll be honest, I had asked Facebook and the church to pray with me. Visiting her in the hospital, she looked like death with all the tubes running in and out of her. I felt that being the big sister, if she had said, "They are going to take a good portion of my lung out," would have scared us to death.

The breath you breathe, you take for granted until you can't breathe. It triggered me to watch my sister with the oxygen mask lying in the hospital bed because I remembered my mother being on oxygen. Not being able to breathe, telling me she loved me through labored breaths, and I remember the last breath. My sister had to undergo physical therapy to learn how to breathe, build her endurance to walk and exercise, and not talk for long periods.

Born in Harlem, she reminded me that she was a fighter. She's not giving up!

Ain't We Lucky We Got Them Good Times

"What doesn't kill you makes you stronger" is the saying I always heard, but losing both my parents made me independent. The hardest part was to open up and communicate. I found that in my sister, I could tell her almost everything. The good, the bad, and the ugly. To listen to her share her most vulnerable experiences for me to learn from, and sometimes I would give her advice too. There were times when we shared poetry, and the rationale behind the thought process gave us a better understanding of the women we were besides being sisters.

Our relationship wasn't perfect; sometimes, we argued and didn't speak. We would eventually miss each other and find a way to call and re-start the conversation like nothing happened.

During the good times, there were plenty when as a family we'd get together and spend time over one another's home. Food was a way to show your love; we loved each other deeply. During the moments when we were gathered, we would always begin by blessing the food. My mother was known for long prayers. So, if a sibling blessed the food and took too long, there was a joke. The nieces and nephews and family friends were invited, and this was our time to fellowship, watch a game on the television and discuss life. Someone always arrived late and would get teased. It didn't matter how old we were. The scenarios were always the same; the feeling of love was there, and there was plenty of laughter.

Barbara, the eldest, was always ready to share advice with the younger generation. She offered opportunities for others behind her to be introduced to programs or organizations to assist with their education and career goals.

Before I made any big decisions, I'd call her. Telling her everything, I was frustrated if she disagreed. But when I stepped out of my way and listened, she had solid facts to support her reasoning.

As a child, I found a way to express myself through words. I would get my cosmopolitan notebook, sit in my room and write about anything. From crushes I had on boys at school, the death of a loved one, to happenings in school. Not knowing it was poetry at a young age, I just knew I loved reading books, watching television, and writing.

In our many conversations when I moved to California after my mother passed, Barbara and I would talk. She said, "I wrote a poem. I'm going to send it to you to give me feedback." I just learned that she also wrote poetry at a young age. We both wrote about past lovers, the hurt we had experienced, dating subjects, and grieving the loss of our mother. Though our styles were different, the core was still the same.

I felt it was in our DNA because my mother became an ordained minister in 1979. Being a woman minister in a male-dominated space, she endured many challenges. She would prepare for her sermons, read her bible, and have her notebook nearby. She wrote her words, recited her scriptures, and preached the Word. Her interpretation of the Bible related to a current situation affecting the congregation. Her words touched people who wanted to change their lives, believed in hope for change, and God using my mother as a vessel to deliver the message. When she passed, we found the journals, envelopes, and bibles with her words scribbled in each.

Words are here forever, even when you're gone. Someone can pick up literature and know what your thoughts are.

I looked forward to having daily conversations with Barbara, telling her about what happened at work, a disagreement I had with someone, and if I met a new love. Hearing how her day went from teaching classes at a local community college, what was happening with her friends, and the saga of dating as you get older.

I loved how our relationship was building, and we were becoming tighter. I learned as a child, I wanted to be like her. Seeing her from afar, not knowing the struggles she endured to accomplish her goals, and later to share photos of places and people we had met years apart, not knowing we'd follow in the other's steps.

She told me a story about when I was a toddler, she took me on a date with her then-boyfriend. Sitting in the car at Burger King, she was eating a whopper and I kept reaching for the burger. Being the big sister and impressing her boyfriend, she said, "Take a bite." My small hands gripped the burger, mouth opened, trying to engulf the whole sandwich in my mouth. She and her boyfriend at the time laughed until they cried because of her quick actions of snatching the burger back. The look on my face, their amazement the toddler would try to eat the whole thing.

Fast forward to December 31. 2006, she and her husband invited me to dinner with them so I wouldn't be alone the day after my mother died. They had reservations at Fat Lady Restaurant in downtown Oakland. Known for its eclectic decor and delicious food. Their orders placed, and the waitress asked what I would like. Per Barbara, it rolled off my tongue like warm butter. "I will have Caesar salad, Kendall Jackson Chardonnay, lobster bisque, rib eye steak well done, baked potato with sour cream, and mixed vegetables. Oh, and I would like a slice of cheesecake. It was my mother's favorite dessert." That look of amazement came into both their eyes. I had no clue they were watching me. All I knew was I had lost my mother. She was my best friend, and food means love. I want to be loved. I want to be comforted. *Damn, I am no longer a toddler, but if you ask, I'll gladly accept and take it.*

Driving home after dinner with full stomachs and listening to smooth jazz on the radio, Barbara told her husband to stop by the

Mormon Temple (Oakland, California Temple). The whole place was decorated with lights visible from Highway 580 East. We took the Harold exit for the temple. Many people visit the temple, and my sister and I were the only African Americans in the place. I strolled up to a man in a black suit and said, "My mother was in Eden Hospital, and her roommate was a Mormon woman. Her husband was a minister, and I wanted to get a message to them that my mother had passed." More men in black appeared surrounding me, asking questions. They then took me to the back, and I'm not even looking back at my sister. I am gone for a while, studying the wall of white men (Mormons) affiliated with the temple. I was asked did I recognize any of them. That's when I realized I was in over my head. I could only remember being at the hospital. The woman's daughter stayed with her, at first, because she was scared of us. As they came to realize my mother was very sick and we weren't concerned about the color of anyone or their beliefs. They warmed up and gave me a gift that I still have. A toiletries bag. When I couldn't recall for the men in the black suits the minister's name whose wife shared a room with my mother, I was escorted back to the lobby. My sister's look on her face said it all. I couldn't wait to get to the car. I said goodbye to the men, went outside to crisp cool air, and got into the car.

My sister said, "What the fuck is wrong with you?" I had frightened her because I'd left her sight. Although she'd wanted to resist becoming the mother figure again, it was there; she would always be my protector.

We had so much in common: our love of documentaries, movies, and the finer things in life. She took the annual Smooth Jazz Cruise, and I sailed on the Capital Jazz Cruise. We would share commentary of what we liked about each new artist that the other had listened to, and plans for the following year.

We also had bad vision, so eyeglasses were a must. We both loved fashionable styles. If I purchased a new pair of Tom Ford eyeglasses, within a month, she got her pair of Prada, and we would admire each other's frames but take notes. *I am going back to get another pair of glasses.* The owner of the optometry office loved the rivalry between the sisters because we were dropping money.

We both loved Mary J. Blige, and I will never forget as long as I live that my sister and I went to the concert together at the Concord Pavilion. We had to have perfect seats to see everything, but not in the front or the back. Right in the middle of Section 205. We are at different stages of our lives relating to the same songs, dancing, and singing along with Mary! Belting out "No More Drama," "Just Fine," and "Stronger" empowered us, making us feel invincible and forgetting all the problems we had to face outside of the pavilion walls. During those hours, we were more than sisters, we were best friends, and I was sharing this moment with my big sister.

The Final Chapter

My father passed on March 12, 1997, and my world froze. I sat on the bed naked, not able to move. I was a Daddy's girl, his princess, and he spoiled me. He had shared so much of his wisdom with me. Stories of his life: born in 1904, and his struggles. Never complaining, the one who encouraged me never to quit, to stay focused, and not to accept mistreatment. He was the first man to tell me he loved me, and when he died eight days before my birthday, I wondered who would have my back. I was then shown that no matter how dysfunctional it may be, my family had my back. No matter my mistakes, they would pick me back up.

When my mother passed unexpectedly in 2006, it was a different feeling. The bond between a mother and daughter can't be compared. I talked to my mother about everything, and she told me when my friends were unreliable, she would always be there, and I could call her at any time. So when she was taken to the hospital, we felt they would find out what was wrong, and she would return home. Our roles of mother and daughter had reversed, and I spoiled her like she was my baby. Before she thought she needed anything, I had already provided it, and it made me feel that I was repaying her for all she had done for me. Since I wasn't blessed with a baby of my own, that God knew I would be the one who would be able to care for her. I was single, self-employed, and would let the gift of discernment take over to guide me. Barbara was there to assist with finding a group home specializing in Dementia/Alzheimer's clients, and she found Center for Elder Independence[3], an all-inclusive care for the elderly located in Eastmont Mall in Oakland. The one-stop facility that would provide care for my mother. Barbara was slowly guiding me to be able to provide support for my mother. She could see firsthand, how I brought her clothing, memorized her medical chart to recite in case of an emergency, and planned my mother's eightieth surprise birthday party.

Barbara strongly believed in not being codependent and would put boundaries up. At times it felt cold and selfish. She later explained that as a child, she had no choice and had to take care of her siblings while her mother went to work to support them. She grew up in a middle-class household, and with the divorce the family moved into the projects. She didn't see her father daily and would have to take the train to visit him in New York. Her childhood was shortened because she had to cook, clean, and delegate chores to her younger siblings. My mother remarried, and Barbara's hopes of reuniting her family stopped on February 29, 1964, when her mother said, "I do" to my father. The family moved from the projects and continued to move to various neighborhoods. The last residence was in an exclusive neighborhood predominantly Caucasian, Jewish, and Polish—professional neighbors of attorneys, doctors, and business owners.

With my mother's passing, Barbara knew my fear of losing anyone else. Promises were made that all were healthy, the longevity of both parents living into their eighties and nineties. There was nothing to worry about. We would be together for a while. For years she had complained about bursitis in her hip, which would sometimes flare up. She would take a Tylenol and be fine soon afterward. On her seventy-fifth birthday, she complained that her knee was bothering her, and I ordered a knee brace from Amazon to be delivered the next day. She was very private and didn't share her ailments with me, but she had made an appointment with her gynecologist. She was spotting blood,

---

3

and they saw a mass. Frightened, she also contacted her oncologist, escalating to have tests done, demanding results. Everyone assured her it wasn't cancer. She went in for a procedure in November to have the mass removed.

In December, 2021, the bursitis flared up again, and her lower back was bothering her. She had so much pain the Tylenol was not working, and she drove herself to urgent care. They took x-rays and told her it was arthritis.

By January, 2022, the pain would travel down her leg, and she took the cane she had used for previous foot surgery out of storage. She used it for stability because the pain would strike, and her knee buckled. As the weeks progressed, she made an appointment with her primary doctor, who diagnosed it was now sciatica. *Sciatica* refers to pain, weakness, numbness, or tingling in the leg. It is caused by injury to or pressure on the sciatic nerve. Sciatica is a symptom of a medical problem. It is not a medical condition by itself."[4] Within weeks it had gotten worse, and she was using a walker. She was my mother's daughter, wasn't accepting the diagnosis, and started sharing it with her family and friends. As her siblings, we were very concerned because she was the healthiest of all the siblings, exercised daily, and got eight hours of sleep. She was making appointments with an orthopedic doctor to examine her and determine what was happening. Her friend had referred her to one of her friends who was an orthopedic surgeon at Stanford Hospital. She made appointments with the doctor at Stanford and also one with Alta Bates. Someone would tell her what was happening and why it was happening so fast.

Both doctors conducted their examinations and gave her materials to read. One prescribed medicine for the pain, and scheduled her return for a follow-up appointment. They felt it was something within the nervous system and wanted to do exploratory surgery. That didn't sit well with us.

Within a few days, she couldn't stand to use the walker and was in a wheelchair to get around the house. She called the doctor at

---

4

Stanford to set a conference call with the doctor at Alta Bates. The doctors had a discussion on a procedure to correct the problem, stop the pain, and she would walk.

February surgery was scheduled, messages were sent out for all to pray, and she called for my sister in Maryland to come to California to assist her when she comes home. She would be hospitalized for two to three days at USF, and life would return to normal. The procedure would go in through her back, and there would be a day to rest before them going back through the front. She asked for blueberry pancakes before having surgery. I utilized DoorDash and ordered breakfast to be delivered for her and chilaquiles for her husband. *Her wish was my command.*

There are calls from her in the evening. She has a beautiful hospital room and a city view. The staff treats her like a queen. Then the calls stop, and days become weeks. The excuse we are given: they are running more tests. Since it is in San Francisco, the only one visiting is her husband, and we are being told a little. No news is good news is the motto!

In March, the sister from Maryland arrived in California with Barbara's husband to pick her up from the hospital. I got the call to collect the eyeglasses she'd ordered. Not thinking much of it, I drive to Oakland, making the usual jokes with the staff that I will be back soon to pick out my glasses. Driving to Barbara's house, I am listening to the radio and happy I will finally see my sister. My brothers' and other sisters' cars were parked out front. I think we must be getting ready to have some type of celebration. I walk up and ring the doorbell, and there is a sad look on Barbara's husband's face. Everyone greets me and tells me to come into the bedroom to see Barbara.

Feeling something is amiss, I feel scared. This is when I transformed into a little girl preparing for the bad news. Sheepishly, I walked into her bedroom and handed her the glasses. She is lying on the bed and looks weak. She motions that I take a seat at the foot of her bed. My brother sits in the chair across from me. My sister closest to me in age is standing behind me, and the sister from Maryland is standing at the door. As Barbara speaks, I look intently to ensure I pay attention because she won't make eye contact. She stares at the ceiling. That is when I see her mouth open, and she tries to contain her emotions, but she has to get it out. When the doctors performed the surgery, they found CANCER! I screamed, and the tears flowed; the sister behind me grabbed me, and I fell into her arms.

Again I am getting news days before my birthday. I am dealing with the impact of cancer, and I am devastated that it is stealing people I love, and I can't stop it. So many thoughts are running through my mind: *I need to take a leave of absence from work and be here to care for my sister. To be in this fight with her.*

I had already booked a trip to Las Vegas, and though I was there, my mind was on my sister. I saved the voicemail from her on my birthday; she is singing "Happy Birthday." I called her, chatted about everything I was doing, the upcoming New Edition concert, and asked if she needed anything. "Not to worry," she said. She's fine, resting and wanted me to enjoy my birthday. Not knowing it would be my last birthday she would be here.

In April, there is another surgery with the hopes that she can walk again by placing a rod in her leg that is dragging. Chemotherapy and radiation treatments are going to be scheduled. When they say it takes a village, we have friends helping, and family members fly in from out of state to assist with her care. While at her home, I overheard her on the phone to her friend say, "Six months," and I pretended not to hear. My other sister comes to visit from Atlanta, and she listens to a visiting nurse talking to my sister; questions are asked, and she is answering what Barbara doesn't want us to know. Always the protector, some discussions with the medical professionals that either Barbara didn't want to accept because she wasn't disclosing everything to us, or she didn't want us to worry.

More physical therapy, occupational therapy, nurse visits, and the effects of chemotherapy treatments were taking their toll.

Again I am trying to provide care, searching the internet what to take for nausea, and talking to everyone for support. I am feeling resistance from her, and I found out from my sister in Maryland Barbara didn't want me to take care of her like I had my mother. She wanted to keep her privacy and independence. Amazon and I had a budding relationship. I would call my sister, and she would mention she had trouble keeping food down; I ordered ginger lollipops. She said she was having a shunt placed in her chest; I ordered a unique shirt to wear to her appointments. I was trying everything to make her comfortable.

As the saying goes, "What doesn't kill you makes you stronger." Well, I found out I wasn't strong. I confided in my job what was happening, and my manager—who was insecure with me in my position—was building a case and trying to get me fired. I had worked remotely for half a day to care for my sister, and she wanted to meet with me immediately afterward. Knowing my emotional state, I asked if it could be on another day. The answer was *yes*, and she kept changing the times. I knew something was up and came to work that Tuesday dressed in a cute Calvin Klein dress, ready to rock and roll for whatever was going to be presented. Within minutes, Human Resources entered the room, and she presented my written warning with false allegations on a large screen. I remained calm, and my mind went into survival mode. I have been down this road before when you have someone in leadership who is not qualified and trying to label you as the "Angry Black Woman." I returned to my desk and worked as usual, sending my documents to my home email, printing my check stubs, and completing my timecard for the rest of the week. That Monday, I saw my doctor, explaining everything that I was dealing with my sister and work, and I was taken out of work on a stress leave of absence.

While I was off work, I took care of myself and let my sister know if she needed anything, I was available. *Anything* she requested, they were delivered. I decided that life was short and I wasn't going to wait until the right time any longer.

I decided I would get a new car. Unsure of what type of car, but I knew I had put it off for my fifty-fifth birthday, and now with

Barbara's prognosis, I wasn't going to wait. I called my bank to get the approval, picked a number out of thin air, and went with it. My other brother-in-law went with me to the dealership to distract them; they always focus on the man and ignore the woman. My sister had already seen a car, the color, and the model on a website and called the dealership to tell them I was coming. The car was on the sales floor, and I knew it was mine after I took it for a test drive. We went to the finance manager's office, where he tried to sell me an add-on, and I called my sister Barbara. I asked what model she had. It was the same. I asked her what dealership she went to. It was the same, and then I asked if she bought any additional add-ons. She answered *no*. Then I drove off the lot with my new car headed to see Barbara from the window. She could see it and asked about all the details. I was so excited to tell her everything. She said, "I want to go for a ride in your new car," but she was too weak to reach the car door.

My other sister lives in the same town as me and could care for Barbara twice weekly. I was given the task of organizing medical bills that were coming in. In comparison, I wanted to help more, but the resistance was increasing, and I couldn't understand why. Also, Barbara was upset with me because she wanted to be the only one to share her condition. I felt helpless I couldn't tell anyone my sister was dying. Our bond was getting weaker, and I needed support too. It had been different when my mother passed; it had been quick. Now only Barbara knew her timetable. Who could I turn to? I am the baby of the family, and secrets were being kept.

By July, Barbara wasn't speaking and not returning my calls. When we talked, she felt I used her to take the leave of absence. It was untrue, but she wasn't hearing anything I had to say. She wouldn't dial my number or speak to me until October.

My sister from Maryland was summoned to come back to help her. Her best friend was also in town, and Barbara wanted her final family portrait to be taken. I received a call to attend and was excited to see my sister. When I saw her, she was laid out on the couch. She had lost so much weight, and the look in her eyes was different. We ate pot roast, potatoes, carrots and peach cobbler for dinner. Then sang "Happy Birthday" and kissed her goodbye on the thirteenth. She was tired and helped back into her room to go to bed.

I had my sister back; I just didn't know for how long.

Running to the Finish Line

Barbara was losing her appetite, eating small quantities of food, not drinking much, and using a wheelchair. She also gave away jewelry to her special friends and family members. Her memory is also foggy, and she has asked her husband to be present if she gives away anything else.

I am searching for another job, interviewing and informing Barbara about it. She is still giving advice on the potential prospects. I told her about a position offered to me at my current employer. I am poker-faced at work, and if asked how my sister is doing, I reply she's okay. I had promised Barbara I wouldn't tell them anything; she advised they were using her illness to get to me.

It seemed like deja vu. *I am reflecting on being a contractor at Pacific Bell Telephone, my father is in hospice, and I need to make more money. The position was a dream position, and I had a panel interview. I received the news and could call my father days before he died to let him know I had gotten the position and would be able to take care of myself and my mother.*

Another call from Barbara; we will be at her home for our final family portrait this time. I have received my offer for a new job with my current employer making more money, working remotely, and receiving a bonus. I told the director to give me time to discuss it with my family.

I arrived at Barbara's, and we prepared for our photo. She came out last, frail and barely standing. We held her up while the photographer took the photos. We settled around the dining room table afterwards.

I present my case regarding the job offer while the siblings chime in and Barbara sits at the head of the table. She asked me to negotiate my offer with the director. I texted the director, accepting the counteroffer on Friday and thanked the director. I had a new job away from the insecure manager, the employees she used to try to set me up, and I was free. Barbara knew I would be taken care of when she was gone. Though she wouldn't be able to continue to protect, legally advise me, or be the sounding board, she knew I was good.

In the following weeks, Barbara was going to have another procedure done. She was barely drinking fluids, her appetite was lessening, and the doctors had said there was nothing else they could do. Her stomach was swelling and gave the appearance of being three months pregnant. They would make her comfortable, and a hospice nurse was assigned to the case. She had called and asked for bed robes so when guests visited she'd look presentable. I also knew she was looking for a sweatsuit for her appointments. Amazon and I became best friends again, and within twenty-four hours, the items were delivered. She loved the sweatsuits and robes. I was spoiling my Queen though she had fought me in the beginning. I knew she was tired now and giving into the fight. I hung the sweatsuits in her closet, kissed her forehead, and left before she went to have her procedure done.

Her husband drove her to the hospital early Friday morning for an outpatient procedure. She came out of the anesthesia and seemed confused. We visited her at her home. Her voice was shallow, and she seemed disoriented. We compensated for the words that couldn't come as we sat and listened to her talk. Sisters know each other, and for words not spoken, we communicated. She was our sister, and she wasn't going to want for anything. We bathed, dressed her, and gave her MAC red lipstick to apply to her thin lips. Her nails were still done from her last visit to the nail salon. She wanted them to be painted black because "that's what young people do," and she would be stylish. We knew it made her feel good; that is all that mattered.

Intuition is where I have said something in my spirit that wasn't right. Come that Sunday, and we were back to visit. We walked into the house, and there was an uneasy feeling. Helping to clean up the kitchen, my sister and I were in protective mode. We took turns; one would heat homemade soup for my ailing sister, and the other would straighten up. We sat in her bedroom and observed her. She ate very little, less than usual. Using the straw to swallow was labored. During this time, she held my hand and said she loved me. She said, "I know I am loved." She looked around the house and saw all I had done. My eyes were welling up with tears that I held back. She saw there were wastepaper baskets throughout the house, liners that I brought for the cans, and when she was sick, there were ginger candies nearby. She was lying in bed with the bathrobe I brought her, looking pretty. She said she felt the prayers that everyone was sending to her. She had lived a good life and had no regrets.

Barbara said she was hot and then she was cold. She called for her husband, who was outside, to assist in changing her underwear. He didn't hear her, so I opened the door to let him know he was needed. She then told me what drawer in her dresser to go to get her underpants while he tried to maneuver the old ones off. She was setting between him lifting and me sliding them on each foot to slide up. She was then sleepy, and I went to the living room to sit with my other sister. We were looking at the photo albums, reminiscing on old times, and knowing we had weeks, if not days, to still have her with us.

As we gathered our belongings to leave, we returned to the bedroom to kiss her goodbye. We walked down the hallways like it was death row because we didn't want to leave her. When we left in our cars, we called each other, saying she didn't look right, and we needed to call the sister in Maryland.

My relationship with God grew closer during this whole time because I was scared, knew what was coming, and was angry. She wasn't supposed to leave me, and she promised me she wasn't going anywhere. I prayed for many days and nights and asked God, "Are you listening? Please heal my sister." My only request. She had beaten cancer before. Why is it not happening this time? Why was someone fine a year before now dying? The cancer had spread through her body like a match to a flame. She had gone from a size fourteen to a size six in months, melting away before our eyes.

As I was watching the television, it was 10:00 pm, and my cellphone was beside me, so I heard it ring once and stop. I looked at it, and it was from Barbara's house. The hair stood on the back of my neck. I immediately called my sister, who lived in the same town as me, told her what had happened, and asked her if she got a call. She said *no*, and while we were trying to figure out what was happening, her phone clicked; another call had come in. She clicked over, and my heartbeat increased while I waited. She clicked back over and said, "Let's roll. Barbara is throwing up blood."

I knew the feeling too well. I jumped in the car, turned on the ignition, and was speeding through the streets of Hayward this time. The last time I had this call was when I lived in San Leandro, and my mother had a stroke, fell, and blood was coming out of her nose.

I arrived at my sister's apartment within minutes, she jumped in, and we prayed. My eyes were on the road, and I was speeding on Highway 580 West this time. I was headed to the Oakland Hills and driving to my sister's dream house, where she looked out to view the San Francisco Bay. The odometer read 100 miles per hour, and my sister in the car was nervous. She called Barbara's husband, who directed us to Alta Bates. The ambulance had just picked up Barbara; they were headed there.

What happened in the seven hours since we saw Barbara? Remember, she didn't look right. Remember, she ate very little. Remember, she was sleepy. *Damn, were these signs right in front of me?* We parked the car, pulled on face masks and scrambled to enter the Emergency Room entrance. Having to go through the metal detector to see all the people waiting. Homeless people who were taken off the streets, people with loved ones waiting to be seen, and us. We rushed over to the desk where the security guard was sitting and asked if my sister was there, an ambulance had brought her in. He answered NO! *How had we beat the ambulance here?*

We waited in the waiting area at the emergency room, praying for my sister and wondering where she was. We kept asking if she was there and being told she wasn't there yet. Minutes turned to hours, security guards changing shifts, her husband arrived, and we sat there silently. Eventually, I went up to the station where the receptionist and security guard sat, explained that it had been hours, and gave my sister's name. They checked and alerted the staff in the back. We could go in the back in groups of two to see her, and being true Betty's kids, we all went back. When we pulled the curtain back, my sister Barbara had aged within hours of when we'd seen her last.

Blood-stained teeth, frail, and with a beanie cap on her head. She looked smaller, darker, and she wasn't speaking. We could sit with her while they prepared a room for her upstairs. She was being admitted. We were asked to leave when the nurse saw us all sitting in the room. We kissed Barbara, told her we would return in the morning, and my siblings and I slowly walked out. That morning driving home, the moon seemed so bright. It lit up the sky; it felt eerie. It felt like we were the only car on the highway. I felt like we were riding into the clouds, trying to stay focused and yet supporting each other. I dropped my sister off, who lived in the same town as me, at her apartment, said "I love you" as she got out and drove on in silence. As I arrived at my place, I felt drained, undressed, and all the emotions poured out. Having a set of clothes ready, shoes prepared at the end of the bed in case I needed to run back to the hospital. I closed my eyes, prayed, and was awakened by the alarm to get ready within hours of getting the call Barbara needed us.

The next day, we each returned to the hospital, giving her name to the front desk to find out what floor she was on—not knowing what to expect when we opened the door. She sat there, letting us hold her hand and kiss her. She could talk, but her voice was almost like a whisper. We sat there in vigil for hours, and the doctors and nurses came and went, checking her vitals. Having small talk with each other. My brother came to sit with us, and the thought that came to my mind was everyone had aged since we went through the ordeal with my mother. He had a cane and walked slower, and I found my attention focused on him. We sat in the room, her best friend asleep on a chair, when she heard Barbara wrestle, she jumped up to attend to her. As the day turned to dusk, it was time for her friend to leave. My brother left soon after, and I followed him without his knowledge, leaning on his cane and trying to remember where he parked his car. As he walked down the hill, realizing his car wasn't there, he crossed the street and found his car. When he opened the door and looked up, I waved as a warrior protecting my own. Now that he was in his car, I turned to go back and check on my Queen to make sure she was comfortable before I left.

On Tuesday, I am back in the parking garage, praying to be strong for her and put on my face mask. I greeted the front desk staff, got my visitor pass, and went to her floor. I came into the room again not sure what I would see. My other sister was already there caring for Barbara, ordering the aides and staff to attend to our sister. I sat down and made small talk and talked to her husband. Then I heard her as clear as day say, "Leave." I asked for clarification. "Who do you want to leave?" She said, "You." My heart sank, I gathered my belongings and left. No one said anything, no defending me, just sat there quietly. Tears slid down my cheeks as I walked through the corridor to the elevator. I am used to hiding my feelings, so I got on the elevator, wiped the tears, and held my head high as I walked out of the hospital. I felt hurt, wasn't welcomed, and hadn't done anything. Then I called my best friend, who explained it wasn't anything I had done. I went home and started cleaning my house. When I am upset, I habitually get that energy out until I am sleepy.

The next day, I was back like nothing had happened. Her health was declining, and she was sleeping more. When she awoke, I said "hello". I was quiet and didn't say a word this time. I was going to sit as quietly as I did when I was a kid and the adults forgot my existence. As the doctors and nurses entered the room, I watched everything and listened for clues. The aides would come and deliver food that she didn't eat. The ability to swallow was fading. She would hold the water in her mouth, and we would say to her gently, "swallow." She was sleeping more, and the television was watching her. As she dozed in and out of consciousness from the medicine, we read magazines and newspapers and took turns leaving to eat downstairs in the cafeteria.

I would stay until visiting hours ended. It was dark, and when leaving, it was my turn to figure out how to find my way into the parking garage, go to the wrong gate, and walk around to find my way inside. Paying for my ticket, I hit the panic button on my car to hear where I had parked it, got into the car, and exhaled. Praying for my sister, gathering myself, and hitting the GPS for home. I pulled up to the gate and inserted the paid ticket for it not to open the gate. I had cars now lining up behind me. Panic striking, horns were honking, and I am stuck. It was an angel in her scrubs, tired from working her shift, getting out of her car and walking up. She saw the look in my eyes and said it was *okay* in a gentle voice. Placing her badge on the reader, and the gate opened. I drove through, thanking her.

It was Thursday, November 17, the sun was shining, and I heard the song while driving to see my sister. She had said her favorite song was from Adele, "Easy On Me," and the tears flowed because I got it. The words struck a chord because by spending time with her and her telling me all her stories directly, I knew what it meant to her.

> "Go easy on me, baby
> I was still a child
> Didn't get the chance to
> Feel the world around me
> I had no time to choose
> What I chose to do
> So go easy on me"[5]

5

I knew she was getting close to the finish line to find her peace, to be her beautiful self and not have to suffer any longer. As I drove the usual route to the hospital, there was a feeling in my gut that it would be soon. I drove to the same parking garage, walked across the street, and was greeted by the front desk staff. My face mask was on and it was time to walk to the elevator; the time to gather my strength and be strong. When I opened the door, she hadn't eaten or drank anything in days. She seemed like a skeleton lying in the bed, her skin so soft. I went straight to her; her eyes weren't closed, but I felt she was still there. She could hear my prayer. Whenever she was scared, she called me to pray and said when I would pray for her, I would wrap my arms around her, and she would lay her head on my breast. She said it reminded her of her mother when she was younger. My mother was a full-figured woman of God, weighing 225 pounds and a size 44 DD bra. A solid woman, those arms pulled you in, and I took pride in knowing I reminded her of Mommy. Right now, it was as if my mom was in the room, and my prayer was for God to have her be comfortable and comfort those in the room and their homes, praying for their sister, auntie, and cousin. When I opened my eyes, my other sister was beside the bed, her hand touching mine, and we were prepared to ride it out. This was the dream I wished I could wake from.

Sitting there, knowing she was leaving me. The woman who I laughed with, shared my secrets and was my advisor. She was more than my big sister. She was my protector. All the hurt she had done to me had long been forgiven. I wished a genie would grant me one wish: live until she was eighty-five years old like she'd promised.

The doctor came and asked that we step out into the corridor so she could give us an update. As the words came out of her mouth, she said her organs were shutting down, and it would be within hours or days. They would make her comfortable.

I knew my Queen B was already gone. We separated and went to digest what was just spoken.

I went into the room where her husband and my siblings sat. We made small talk, and it changed as the plan was to ride it out. We kissed Barbara goodbye. I said, "I love you" knowing I wasn't coming back. This time I left the hospital knowing it was the last time I would see my sister. I found my car this time with no problem. I got in, pressed the GPS *Home* and drove out.

On November 18, 2022, I got up and drove to work. Everyone was shocked that I was there, walking on eggshells around me, not knowing what to say. I stayed busy, not telling anyone what was happening and praying to make it through the day without crying. My coworkers asked me to go to lunch; I accepted and said I would drive. I received the call when I drove into the parking lot of the cafeteria and answered. They listened to the words over Bluetooth, and I wasn't by myself this time. My sister crossed the finish line. She was free!

Now to pick up the pieces of my broken heart.

Now What?

Now what do you do? Your loved one has passed. Were you a caregiver? Were they your sibling, parent, family member, or friend?

Did you have feelings of being lost? Angry? Guilty? Acceptance?

Bereavement is the grief and mourning experience following the death of someone important to you. While it's an inevitable part of life—something that virtually all of us go through at some point—losing someone you love can be one of the most painful experiences you'll ever have to endure."[6]

There was a difference between losing my father, who was ninety-two years old and battling prostate cancer, which he expressed four years prior. He wouldn't be here always. It was the preparation of knowing that one day it would happen. I had moved to California and came home to visit but didn't notice anything significant that would give me warning signs. The cancer had spread, and he had to have a procedure to remove some of his intestines. He declined after that, and within three months of being in hospice, he passed before I could return to Connecticut. I felt shocked, I wondered who would protect me, and I was a Daddy's girl. So there was a hole in my heart. Seeing him lying in the casket, he wasn't recognizable, so I felt acceptance. I knew he wasn't suffering anymore, I had memories of him well because I didn't see him transition, and I knew the legacy lives on.

With my mother, we knew she had Dementia; then it went to Alzheimer's. The doctors were changing her medication, we had a family meeting months before, and she complained of shortness of breath. We were hopeful that when she was admitted to the hospital, they would find out what was wrong; she had said that she couldn't walk six feet without being able to catch her breaths and she would be home for her favorite holiday... Christmas. There were tests, MRIs, and oxygen while she was in the hospital for weeks. We didn't expect to be told that our mother was dying, she wasn't coming home, and we had two days. The autopilot turns on; we're running back and forth to the hospital and preparing for a funeral on the East Coast. That Friday, we surrounded her, sang gospel hymns, and she was happy. She didn't look like someone dying within hours, but the morphine kicked in, her eyes closed, and we focused on helping her transition. We had no time to think about ourselves. I was numb and felt that I had gone through the motions until I returned to California. I felt a sense of guilt, thinking, would she still be alive if I had taken her to the hospital her primary doctor told me to? I felt I was doing the best for her by having her taken to the best hospital in the Bay Area. I then went through all the emotions of denial, anger, and depression, and only years later, I felt acceptance. I could listen to others, realizing that Alzheimer's had taken over and the body was responding. After her death, I would sob, place her nightgown on and look at her pictures. My desire to eat was the last thing on my mind, and I had to seek a nutritionist's assistance because I could go for hours not eating. I had no will to live, impacting my job as a sole proprietor. I couldn't support myself. I was also asking God how he could let this happen. I donated her clothes, medical equipment and distributed her belongings to my siblings. This was a different feeling of grief than my father's death. Both were traumatic, but losing my mother at eighty unexpectedly, I am still dealing with grief, and it has been seventeen years. I had support from the church members where I was a member at that time, calling, praying, and getting me out of the house, but they didn't know everything I was dealing with.

I have lost other siblings to cancer who lived on the East Coast, and the loss was dramatically different. I cried when I received the news of their passing and sent sympathy cards and money. I checked on my nieces and nephew, but the grief didn't hit the same.

Losing Barbara, I am in disbelief. I had bonded with her; I went over all the ailments she mentioned and surgeries and questioned other siblings who had talked to her to see if they had answers. And I wanted to sue doctors. I felt they were to blame. How can someone who takes tests every year to ensure the cancer didn't come back have cancer now in other parts of their bodies but not their lungs?

How could they not see she had cancer and it reached Stage 4? Did she already know and keep it from us? All these questions were running in my mind, *could I have saved her?* I had times when I was overwhelming her with wanting to care for her. I was scared and wanted to give her the same amount of care I gave my mother. She refused my help and would stop talking to me for months. She told another sibling that she didn't want me to care for her like I had others and chose another sister to care for her. The clock was still ticking, and I only had a few months to spend with her. I knew the last time I saw her, she was gone, and didn't want to see her take her last breath. Then regret it, feeling ashamed that I wasn't there to support my siblings and see the funeral home come to take her away. She was the first person I knew that wanted to be cremated. The day she was cremated, there was a stillness in the air. Her husband wanted to know if we would accompany him to the crematorium after the three-day waiting period. The answer was NO!

Her service would take place a few months later to give the family time to come after the holidays. So the time preparing wasn't rushed. We were grieving, sometimes picking up the phone to call her, realizing she was gone. I was determined to share pictures of her from my photo albums. My house looked like a tornado had hit. My eyes were bloodshot from crying. It felt like being in a fog and this would hit like slamming into a wall. Sometimes I was excluded, and glad my siblings were adamant that I was included.

Sitting at the memorial service, we all had on her favorite color, purple, and paid tribute to her and her life.

We sat in our birth order as we did at my mother's funeral. The memories started flooding in. Listening to friends, coworkers, and family members share memories took the band-aid off, and all the feelings I had bottled up, I cried that day. Comforting each other and being on guard for what would happen next.

I couldn't grieve as usual because people were playing with our inheritance. Taking inventory of her possessions and ensuring it was evenly distributed was the final task that still wasn't settled. I had to put my wall up and protect my heart. Then I pushed everything to the back and prepared to pledge for a sorority, so I kept busy. Once in a while, I would post on Facebook and Instagram when it would hit me. I have not moved to acceptance yet. Friends who were close to the family were now distant. The ending feels incomplete.

I decided to celebrate my sister's life by writing in the journal. I am trying to hold onto her memory. I miss her so much. The emotions sometimes float over me like a thundercloud, and the tears flow as the words are written.

Poetry was what we had in common; it was poetry's mission to heal a broken heart.

Letting go

I don't want to forget you is a thought we all struggle with. Going through the stages of grief, it doesn't matter if it is weeks or years.

Facebook memories pop up, and I post it on my feed. I was sharing the moments, returning in time, and remembering Barbara.

I have blocked out all feelings, distancing myself from my siblings and using excuses to avoid closure. Let me stay busy, find new projects, and lose myself, so I won't be able to face what it is.

Friends are checking on me, asking how I am doing. I am putting on that imaginary mask that I became familiar with and saying I am fine. I will never forget when Barbara went to the doctor, she had endured chemotherapy and radiation. They were going to let her know if the cancer was shrinking. We were all hopeful, but when Barbara said the doctors had done everything and nothing else could be done, she had made her acceptance. The calmness she presented in her voice made me take inventory of my life. How can you see your life flash before you know your time is ending without knowing the day or hour? For someone in control of everything in her life, not knowing how the ending will play out. The first time returning to my job after she had passed, I updated my emergency contacts, and reality hit.

This was going to be the new normal. How much my life was intertwined with hers when decisions had to be made; realizing she would not answer the call, I took a deep breath. Let's go!

The big sister in the parental role was gone, the safety net disappeared, and I had to step out on faith. I had lost loved ones before, and I lost myself before. I was left to hang out to dry, and I almost gave up. This time was going to be different.

I read an article that inspired me. "Before you can let go of grief, you must spend ample time with it. Letting go of grief isn't something that can be done in a few weeks time. You must first allow yourself time to mourn, cry, anguish, and long for your loved one."[7]

It took me forty years to accomplish my dream of pledging to a sorority, and I almost talked myself out of the opportunity. My special angel was looking out for me this time with the timing. So immediately when I realized the process, I had to deal with what I had been running from. I had told my siblings I couldn't talk to them during the process when I had free time. I didn't spend it with them because I didn't want the conversation to come up. I hadn't mourned the loss of my sister. I jumped from getting a new job in November, writing a book, and pledging a sorority, and it was now May. It was time to put in the work.

1. Take care of myself if it meant I had to set boundaries in all relationships
2. Travel the world (writing a wish list)
3. Open up and talk to someone about getting through grief
   a. This was difficult, and I knew I had to start with the first step of trusting someone to listen, not be judgmental, and let me get it out
4. Taking responsibility for my own life and the decisions I make

The process hasn't been easy, but by removing myself from situations and sitting in my feelings. Letting the tears flow, talking about Barbara before she was sick and the good times. Letting go of the anger that she was to be here still. Being proud of the woman she

---

7

was, understanding that even in the end she was protecting her family, keeping secrets until the last breath.

I realized that in December, when I took an impromptu solo trip to Monterey to understand her final wishes to have her ashes spread there. I understood she was at peace, and I have to continue to live my life.

I have to take everything she shared with me and continue to be strong and recognize my self-worth; she knew I loved her and was proud of me.

Ashes to Ashes

"Absence from the body present with the Lord"
I could accept you were leaving me, but I wasn't ready for the next phase.
There would be no viewing of the body,
No picking out the casket,
No picking out the outfit you would wear.
Then I drove to where you wanted your ashes to be spread
As I stood on the embankment
Seeing the stillness of the water,
The sky blue,
The air is fresh,
The tears flowed
Ashes to Ashes, dust to dust in sure, and confident hope of the resurrection to eternal life.
Purple
The color of royalty.
It was my mother's favorite color.
When she passed, I found a ring and was drawn to the color.
I bought it, placed it on my finger, and wore it daily.
I bought a suit that was purple too. I wore it for essential meetings because the feeling of authority, ancestors, and my mother's spirit made me feel unstoppable.

It was only natural that I noticed a change from my favorite color to now it's purple.
I am a Queen
I am a child of the King

Purple

Purple was her favorite color
Representing royalty
Purple Sunday outfits
Purple hats
It wasn't always my favorite color
After she died, I found I was drawn to it
Purple rings
Choosing a crayon color
Purple
When my sister found love
Her gown was purple
When my sister died
Her photo on the program
She had the wedding photo with the purple gown
The family wore purple
It took on a different meaning
I place the purple ring back in the jewelry box
It doesn't feel like a favorite anymore.

No More

No more pain
No more suffering
No more bills
No more pills
No more doctors
No more treatments
No more hospitals
No more false hopes
No more cancer.

The Last Day

I saw the look in your eyes
You were looking through me like you were seeing past me to your
destiny
I recognized that look
I saw it before
I knew it wouldn't be much longer.
I held your hand, and the warmth had gone
Your last day here on earth
My heart breaking into pieces
The feelings flooding
The tears welling up in my eyes
Kissing your cheek
Saying goodbye on...
Your last day!

On A Journey

Decided at the last minute
Curious to find your resting place
Driving along the coast
On a journey
The scenery is breathtaking
Seeing the water stillness
The seagulls and ducks
The smell of the air is even different
I got a view of having the sunrise awaken me
Walking along the trail
Stopping to take it all in
The sailboat floats effortlessly
It was then that the tears flowed
I understood

Water

Transparent
Tasteless
Odorless
Colorless
Yet vital to our survival
I watched as she could not swallow
Holding it in her mouth
Confused about what to do
The plea in her eyes
I begged, "swallow."
Her whispers answered

Akousa

She came back from her trip to Ghana
Excited by the new name Akousa
It means a girl born on a Sunday
Yearning to help others
Seeing her crown wrapped
Wearing traditional Ghanaian female dress
Listening to her stories
Seeing the pictures
Meeting the students
She had found her true purpose
She was the elder of our tribe
As a true leader
A warrior
Elegance
Queen
She was home

Rain

Rain...
The cleansing of the earth
Standing under the gray skies
Arms extended out
Head tilted back
Eyes closed
Letting the rain cleanse me
All the pain
All the suffering
All the toxicity
I am one with the earth
Lord, cleanse me

Love Is

Love is pure
Love is kind
Love is looking into a newborn's eyes
Love is wanting to be in your presence
Love is feeling like you can't breathe without you
Love is letting go
Love it welcoming you back in
Love is knowing you're loved
Until death do us part

Hold Me

In the midnight hour
When the chill hits my skin
I quiver from the temperature
Snuggle close
Please hold me
Don't let me go
Make me feel secure
When the world is unforgiving
Let me know if it's going to be okay
Please hold me

Cancer

Hiding in dark places
A game of hide and seek
Waiting to take the throne
Cancer doesn't just attack the body
It attacks the family as well
The tears flow
The doctor's visits
Comforting the loved one
Cancer eating away
Taking away the appetite
Eating away at the body
The pain increases
The agony doesn't subside
Promises of surgery
The mystery of if it has gone
The screams for forgiveness
Let it end is the request
Cancer is sitting there laughing
Waiting to take the final bow
Their eyes close
The breath ceases
The final curtain closes

Knock Knock!

For nine years, you were escaping the inevitable
Every year tests ran, and you were free
You thought!
Knock Knock!
Who's there?
CANCER
More tests are run
More operations
Take it out is the plea
Too late
Knock Knock!
Who's there?
Death

Sisters

We were born of the same bloodline
We shared so much in common
We were each other comforters
We shared laughter
When we had a tear shed, the other was there to wipe it away
The daily calls
The visits where we sat in silence and just breathe
There are times I want to pick up the phone and call
I hear your voice on the voicemail
I looked at the cards sent
I will always miss you and hold onto the memories
that we once shared

The Ring

He gave her a ring that symbolized their love
She wore it proudly, and when she said I do
it was sealed with a kiss
Fast forward, they had a child that made the family
The three musketeers were seen everywhere together. She always
wore the ring and had it embellished with more diamonds, making
it unique. It was the simple band that made the union complete
When she died, the ring was to go to the only child from the union,
but it was taken for ill intent
The child grew into a patient woman waiting.
The promise what was rightfully hers would be gifted when the taker
passed
The taker had a change of heart after fifteen years of flaunting it in
front of the patient woman
A call came, "Come to get the ring."
Cries and screams were heard.
The ring was placed on the finger, and the circle was complete. Both
rings are where they belong.

To be Loved

We crave the special someone to look at us from across the room, and butterflies leap in our stomachs.

From exchanging glances to having small talk and conversations for hours that seem like seconds.

We all want that special feeling. To constantly look at your phone for the next call, the walks in the park, and, yes, that first kiss.

There is that feeling of wanting to be around that person. Not in a smothering way, but to be in their presence brightens our day!

When you hear the first time I love you, and you say it back, there is that connection. You hope that it is accurate as you let your guard down to your heart.

The feel of the arms caressing you and letting you know you're safe and protected.

Protected so that you can be yourself, be silly, or cry and know it is safe.

We all want that; only a few conquer it and keep it until death do you part.

Warrior

Eyes mahogany brown
Skin glistens with sweat on her brow
Hair braided in an intricate style to show us where to go
Walking ever so gracefully with the intent to pivot at any moment
Her physique sculpted
She is a warrior
Trained to protect her tribe
Fighting until her last breath
Conquering whatever the world tries to throw
Leading the pack
Demanding the respect she deserves
She never took her eyes off of her surroundings
Fighting off predator
Training the young to take over when she's gone
Warrior

Love Letters

Love letters
Eloquently written
An expression of the love we shared
Wants, Needs, and Desires
Spelled out on each line
Anticipation for the next to arrive
Letters opened quickly
Reading each page
Memorizing each line
Promises of forever
Words scribbled on scented pages
Laughs, tears, and lust
Placed gently into the envelope
Sealed with a kiss
Sent between lovers
Love letters...

Promises

Oh how my heart still burns. Longevity is what you thought you had. You had a long life to live, but neither of us knew the outcome. Like a sip of poison, it entered your body and slowly took over. No one recognized the changes in your body. The aches and pains you thought were nothing were the silent killer.

I remember the words coming out of your mouth in slow motion. The years you thought you had were months; I would be left again. The birthday wishes I saved on my phone. The pictures I looked at it and asked if this was a dream. The tears slowly streamed down my cheeks, and my vision became blurry. You held my hand, and I felt the cold setting in.

The last breath you took, I couldn't be there to see because reality had hit, and I understand that promises were meant to be broken!

I Remember

Excited about your return home
Not realizing all was there
Gather in your bedroom
Your demeanor was different
A chill entered the room
I felt I had transformed back in time
As I sat on your bed
I was no longer an adult but a child sitting and waiting
You gently spoke to me
Trying to gather your thoughts
"They found cancer" were the words that escaped your lips
As they traveled across to my ears
I saw your lips move
The words hit like a bullet piercing my heart
As I screamed, arms surrounded me to catch me
The tears flowed from your eyes
Tears flowed
My breathing labored
I asked God, "Why?"
I remember
The room
Who was there
Your smell

Your eyes
It was March 12ᵗʰ, 2022
It was deja vu
I am finding out you're dying
Was it a nasty prank?
My father had died twenty-five years earlier on this date
Yes, I remember!

Sister's Keeper

Sisters have a bond like no other
We are each other's best friends
We are each other's clothing stylists
We are each other's therapists
When everyone turns their back, they are there
They are your first cheerleader
When hungry, they feed you
When one takes a beating, we all take the beating
Doesn't have to be biological to be a sister
It could be a stranger in distress
We come to the rescue
When asked, "Are you my sister's keeper
Without thinking, the answer is…
Sister's Keeper

Spirit Leaves

I knew the look very well
The look in the eyes where they are gone
I remember seeing her on her birthday before knowing what would
happen
I saw her sitting in the chair, and she gazed out into the scenery
It was at that moment I felt in my gut she was leaving
It was eleven months later
I walked into the hospital room
My hand lightly touched her head
Her eyes looked beyond me
I whispered, "I love you."
When a loved one is preparing to transition
I wonder what that look means
Do they see loved ones who have gone before them?
Are they already dead?
Is this the shell that is lying there?
The lifeless look will forever be a look I never want to see
I saw it before, and I want to close my eyes not to see it again

Shake What Your Momma Gave You!

My last memory I'll never forget.
I had mentioned to her, the one in the family that couldn't dance
How I had struggled to learn a new dance
She is the oldest and laughed at the youngest
She says, "You're thinking too hard about it."
Being the big sister, she always guided, taught, and sometimes scolded me.
She was going to show me how to do this dance!
She turned up the music and danced!
In disbelief, I followed and did it!
Smiling, I felt like Momma was smiling from above
Momma is proud of herself as a dancer
Showing us, as kids, the dances she used do
Tell us about the contests she and her brother won
I am now sitting here by myself, reflecting
Both women who inspired me have gone
When the opportunity arises
There I am on the dance floor

If I Ever

Watching someone slowly die makes you reflect on your life.
You start making different choices
You write out your bucket list
You look at your finances,
Want to make sure you got your will intact
Scheduling doctor appointments to make sure your health is up to par
No hidden illness
You don't want the doctor to tell you that you have months to live
Sadly you're getting everything in order so that those left behind don't have to suffer
The words If I ever get the chance, I will do…
It hits differently when you know someone close is dying
Life isn't promised
It's a wake-up call
You never know when it is your last stop
You want to live each moment and open your heart
Feeling guilty
Don't wait to enjoy life
If I ever …is now!

Bus Ride

At eighteen years old, she is leaving it all behind.
Ready to fulfill her dreams
Leaving the small town
Her siblings, she was the second Momma to
Tears shed
She was a Daddy's girl
Divorce is a sad experience for anyone, but especially the eldest
Stepfather wasn't to take his place
Never going to call him Pop
Graduating high school and going to be eight hours away
Seeing all the scenery as the bus passes by
Anxious for what would be there
No more babysitting for her
There wasn't anger as some might try to portray
She was going to be free
It was the passage of becoming a woman
All the accomplishments
All of the sacrifices
Because she took the leap made it easier for those behind her
Times it was lonely
Times there wasn't enough money
If she hadn't taken the bus ride
She wouldn't be the woman she is today

Snatch the Bandage Off

When you're hurt
you put a bandage on
Let it heal and feel better
With grief, you go
Through the phases
Of denial, fear, anger, and acceptance
Every anniversary
Every birthday
Mother's Day
Father's Day
The triggers happen
The tears flow
Feeling of depression
The closure reopened
Saying goodbye
The feeling is like
"Snatching the bandage off."
And it hurts like hell

Hey, Baby

Seeing him across the room
Eyes meet, and look away
Both of us are shy, but intrigued
We speak briefly and exchange numbers
He baked warm oatmeal cookies to give me each time we saw each
other
I don't know if I am anticipating the cookies or seeing him
Wondering if we are just friends or if we will take it further
As we walk out into the evening
He grabs my hand
I feel secure as he leads
Next is the kiss
I say, "Hey, Baby."

Travel

As a child, your dream was to travel the world
Read about exotic places
See places in movies and on television
Make bucket lists of places to go
Take the first trip
Let the breeze go through my hair
Take in all the scenery, cold or hot
Taking pictures
Saving memories
Tasting the foods of the locals and exploring the spices, tastes, and smells
When I am old, I will reflect on my adventures and traveling!

Ain't Nobody

Ain't Nobody
You can't tell someone to change unless they want to change
Ain't Nobody
Love you like your mother
Ain't Nobody
Going to tell you
You're wrong when you're right
Ain't Nobody
Going to love you better than yourself

My Life in the Sunshine

Looking at someone before they pass
Life flashing before you
All the good times
The bad times
Listening to the stories
Cruising the world for thirty days
Seeing the sunsets
Writing the memories on pages
She grabs my hand
She knows her days are numbered
She says I have traveled the world
I have lived my best life
I have no regrets
I have lived my life in the sunshine

Pass the Torch, Sis

Coming from a lineage of bad mama jammas
Brick house
Coke bottle figures
Big breasts
Small waist
Junk in the trunk
From the time we can remember
We loved men, and they loved us
Sharing stories about what we did, how we did it, and where
They were tall, short, slim, and thick
There was always that one
The one who could call you in the middle of the night
You would wake up and hear his voice on the other end of the receiver
"I want you."
And the response would be, "Come on."
Jump in the shower, and use the Bath & Body body wash to smell good
Lather and make sure every part of you is clean
Lotion and have the skin smooth
Ready for whatever was coming through the door
Throw on some Marvin Gaye
Light the scented candles
The rest was history
In the morning after he left

I would pick up the phone to share my stories
You would tell me yours and give me tricks to use the next time he
came over.
Your playbook was for champions
You said you had retired
You had taught me all you knew
The torch was passed
I would now have to revise the playbook
I would have to share it with those coming up behind me
So I would call them and tell them the tales of your younger days
What to do or not to do
Smile when they called to give me their results
Thinking of the one who wrote the book

Pieces of Me

Each time a loved one leaves
They take a piece of me
I want to hug you tight and not let go
Walls go up
Got to protect my heart
I need you to be here
I am selfish
I know that you must eventually leave
Some leave unexpectedly
Some I expect
It's not fair
As they depart
I feel a part of me leaving
I feel like a jigsaw puzzle
Another piece I am looking for
Can't put me back together again
There are pieces of me lying on the floor
Scattered
Lost forever
There won't be nothing left of me
They are slowly leaving me

Life is the Sentence

Standing in front of my peers
Begging for forgiveness
For all the wrongs I have ever done
I promise I will be good
I won't be late
I'll show up
I will listen to you as you speak
I won't cut you off
You want to go to
Brunch? Church? Vacation?
Just promise you won't leave
I promise we won't end the evening mad at each other
Promise I'll tell you I love you before we hang up
Just don't leave me alone
I don't want to be here by myself
They each shake their heads
Silly rabbit tricks are for kids
The judge taps their gavel
The sentence is read
They get to ascend into the clouds
"You get to stay."

Red Lipstick

I don't know what it is about; it is
As a woman applying the red lipstick
Upon my thick lips
Looking at myself in the mirror
Pucker up
Blow a kiss to myself
You're beautiful
Sexy
Intelligent
Can conquer anything that is thrown at me
Walking to the door, a final check
Watch out, world, here I come!
With my red lipstick
Catching his eye
Batting my eyes
Playing coy
He doesn't know
This red lipstick is about to be smeared
It doesn't matter if it is matte, high gloss, or whatever
I am better now with my
Red lipstick

He Only Beats Me
on Friday (Pt.2)

She defends him
He was stressed
I provoked him
I should have had dinner ready
The kids are screaming
I should have put them in bed before he got home
Bruises hidden
The black eye behind the Chanel shades
Silent tears
You told one
They told another
Promise don't tell anyone
Think about the kids
It got to the one
The call came
Leave was the plea
She says she doesn't have any place to go
The one says I just wrote a check
I can pay your rent
I can buy you a house

The tears are heard through the receiver
She replied, "he loves me."
Love doesn't hurt
She makes more excuses for him
The one screams let me help you
You're not alone
The sad response before she hangs up
"He only beats me on Friday."
Today is Thursday
I got one more day
I'll be okay
The feeling of the one is helpless
Memories she can relate to
She picks up her pen
And lets the words flow
She sealed the envelope
The testimony on the pages
The secrets of her past
Hoping to send strength to her

Love Me

Loving the skin you're in took time
Growing up being teased for the dark melanin
People are baking in the sun
Risking skin cancer to get the golden color brown
As she matured
Finding the beauty in her eyes
Loving her figure
Her skin is flawless
No one could guess her age
She grew into herself
And during the '60s sported her afro
She was a true queen
One that demanded respect
She walked with a graceful purpose
When she looked in the mirror if there were any insecurities
They were never shown
All we saw was perfection
Wrapped in a coco brown complexion
Seeing her reflection
She was pleased with what she saw
Beautiful coco brown skin she was once ashamed of
Now she was loved

Feelings

Feelings
Some wear them on their sleeves
Others hide them
There are feelings of joy
There are feelings of sadness
As I sit here, I turn on the record player
Listening to Kenny Rogers's version of "Feelings."
This is not the same.
I have so many feelings pinned up,
Trying to figure out what I will do now.
I can go through photos albums for hours,
Replay you singing "Happy Birthday" and saying "I love You."
How I wish I could turn back the hands on the clock,
Hold you one more time,
Laugh at your bad jokes,
Tell you about my dreams
Listen to you. Give me the playbook
Oh, how I miss you
These feelings are getting the best of me

A Letter to You

Hey, Sis,

I wanted to write you and let you know that I miss you every day. I am keeping myself busy. We had daily calls for updates on what was happening in the world, the family, and you. Realizing we had so much in common besides eyeglasses, we loved being around people, especially younger ones. The calls for me to translate slang, what you heard your students saying, and how I told you I was singing a song at work without knowing the meaning.

We love traveling, sharing photos, and discussing our next adventure. Where did we get that desire from?

There is so much that I want to say. There are so many questions I have.

What is it like?

Have you seen Momma?

There was so much I still had to share with you

You were to go for a ride in my new car

Everyone misses you, especially me

Morality seemed so distant before, and now we are all scared

You were the one to keep us calm

I miss the smell of you in your house. It's slowly fading

I saw your slippers placed under the bed, where you left them last, waiting for you to put your pedicured toes back in

I miss you saying, "What's up, buttercup."

Signed,

Your Sister

Crying

Crying for you
I still feel the warmth of your body
I can still hear your voice
Telling me what to do next
Thinking about you
Hearing a song, and I think this was your favorite
Sometimes, unexpectedly, the tears start
Placing a piece of your jewelry on
It doesn't look the same on me
Going to your house
It feels empty
Walking back to your bedroom, expected to turn the corner and see you
Disappointment slides in when I realize you're gone forever
They say to hold onto the memories
I would rather have you
As I wipe away the tears

Life Afterwards

It has been months since you passed, and life is supposed to return to normal. Easier said than to do it. We seem out of sync because you're the oldest, and we are trying to figure out how to pick up the pieces. Where do we fit now?

We hold onto each other tighter and are scared to let go, like a child separated from a parent. You were the parent when they were absent. As we age, we still need you to discuss health issues, relationships, and raising children. Who is supposed to fill your shoes?

Going into places you frequented takes a lot of effort.

I went to get my eyes examined by the optometrist we both went to.

The tears flowed uncontrollably, and hugs from the doctor and staff. They sat with me and reminisced about our rivalry with purchasing glasses and shared laughter. Handed a bouquet to make me feel better, but it won't replace you.

Calls to other siblings, and they share how they're struggling too. Missing conversations on various topics is not the same as talking to others.

I decided that I was going to take the first step. I am going, not going to forget you, but I am going to live my life with no regrets. Planning my bucket list of accomplishments I want to achieve—planning trips and getting excited to travel the world. I remember you placed a world map in your kitchen of places you had traveled, and as usual, I am following your steps.

Taking the first step, scared that I would fail, and then I did it! I traveled by myself, and I thought about you each step of the way. The thrill of flying above the clouds, wondering what the destination would be like now. Knowing I couldn't call you to tell you about it, then a breeze touched me. A smile came across my face. Spend time by myself looking out at the ocean, thinking about where I want to go next. Set the alarm clock to wake up to see the sunrise, meditated on the balcony, felt the sadness slowly faded and wrote down the next goal I wanted to accomplish, the dream of empowering returned to me. Coming from a long lineage of strong African American women, we still feel fragile, unworthy, and looked over for positions we are qualified for. I think about my mother once working as a maid cleaning people's houses to her determination to one day live across the street from the place she cleaned many years before. She didn't share her dream for fear of being told she couldn't.

Listening as a child to conversations about women who wanted to start businesses, get an advanced degree, and share resources. It was planted there in my spirit, and I didn't know what to do with it until now!

As a certified public accountant teaching accounting at Contra Costa Community College, I thought about you.

You taught students who were single mothers, entrepreneurs, and those wanting to start a business. You saw how they needed resources and developed a course curriculum, got funding, and taught the fundamentals of running a business and beating the odds of failing within a year. Listening to you share years later, about your son-in-law wanting to start his own business, and he didn't know your background when giving him advice—his surprise when you presented him with the playbook given to your students. You were always helping others and knew your purpose.

In 2012, I began going to Utah as a travel agent on a familiarization trip and continued going annually. I would unplug from all distractions, meditate, and converse with other women there. It was the feeling when I boarded the plane to return, letting me know I felt different and wanted other women to feel the same way. I didn't know how to approach it, but I took one step at a time; it would happen one day. Let me start putting my playbook together.

While writing my books and going on tour, more supporters shared their stories with me and told me my stories had to be shared with others. The idea was to become a motivational speaker. I traveled in July 2019 to become a certified life coach for Women's Issues & Diversity in Louisville, Kentucky. I entered an intense workshop, prepared outlines, and was excited to apply the teachings. The following year, I was honored to speak at the University of California, Berkeley Campus afterward. Then the pandemic happened and put the dream on the back burner.

Well, it's time to turn the burner up and figure out how to help women feel empowered—a way for me to heal myself and give back to others. For years I hosted brunches selecting various women with different backgrounds to share their experiences, network, and build friendships. I realized I had the best role models in my mother and sisters.

1. To lift her by pouring powerful, inspirational affirmations into her. I knew since I was a child that I was loved. I learned to apply myself from my father. The feeling of self-esteem was strong, and I felt that when I had forgotten who I was, it impacted me. When I thought I was alone and isolated myself, I sat in my feelings. So having a system circle of friends and others to support, I had the sounding board. Sharing my story helps others who have experienced something similar. Standing flat-footed and looking in the mirror, knowing I am confident, not settling, and my self-worth.

2. I was stepping out of my way! We are our own worst critics. I shared earlier how I had a dream for something I wanted for over forty years. I had been turned down three times, and the negative thoughts entered my being. I shared it with a few people, so I talked myself out of not applying when the opportunity came knocking. Then as I was preparing her memorial, I came across a photo my late sister had sent me. It reminded me that I needed to put the negative thoughts out of my mind. Whenever the thoughts creep in, I now play music, see myself on the other side of the negative, and stay positive. "I can do all things through Christ that strengthens me."[8]

3. Support Her Dreams! - My mother was an entrepreneur from selling Avon, owning a group home for mentally challenged women, and other endeavors. My sister was a certified public accountant. She had a custom gold jewelry business. So it was only natural that I became an entrepreneur having multiple businesses. How can I support other sisters? Supporting women-owned businesses by spreading the word, purchasing their products, seeking their input on where they need help. I have mentored aspiring authors who had dreams of writing. I have contacted other women inviting them to showcase their businesses on a global platform. I was helping them to fulfill their vision and not for ego but knowing that we all win and you have to reach back to help.

4. Get that paper! Always learning to increase your knowledge and skill set. Learning something new is something no one can take away from you at any age. I was enrolling in classes online and receiving certificates or degrees. I have doubted my ability, thinking I wasn't worthy, and would panic when finding courses. Then the amazement was that I loved to challenge myself, receive the certificate and apply the knowledge. Not to say that the self-doubt feelings would never come but challenging myself to learn something new

---

8

was to better myself. From getting my Master's, receiving a license to sell insurance, and becoming a certified travel agent. I was scared and, sometimes, wanted to give up, but knowledge is power. Go for it!

5. Giving Back! Volunteering is a beautiful way of giving back to your community. Being able to find what you're passionate about and volunteer. The feeling of helping another person or organization takes the focus away when I am feeling depressed or grieving. Not that I ever want to forget my loved one, but I want to help someone; the result is I have helped myself. Gratification is joy. I was asked in March to speak at a middle school for their Career Day. Sharing my childhood experience, education, and what I do as a professional. Seeing the light in their eyes, asking questions and being able to inspire them to dream for their futures. I know my sister, the educator, is smiling down at me.

6. Being Open and Honest! This was the hardest challenge for me to open up and talk. Talking about the feelings that were bottled up about losing my sister, questioning how long she knew, questioning her actions the previous year regarding ailments. Typical feelings along the grievance path and trying to find acceptance. Using a journal to write them all down and then talking with my best friend. Times I would call, cry and not say anything. I had held my feelings in since learning my sister told me she had cancer, when she passed, and months later after her memorial service. Keeping myself busy to feel numb until April and it hit like a cannon ball. My calendar had cleared and I had time to feel the pain. Opening up was the best step forward. I had to be honest with myself.

I made a promise to myself to live my life because tomorrow isn't promised. I have updated my will removing my sister. Being a daughter of a minister I know that there is a heaven, there is also comfort in knowing that Barbara is in a better place because the pain and suffering she endured, she is now free. I found myself being selfish. I never thought she would be gone, She promised she had ten more years at least. Promises are meant to be broken and forgiveness is to be had. As I stand at the Monterey Fisherman's Wharf, looking out at the still water, ducks floating, and a small sailboat in the far distance a tear rolls down my face. Saying Goodbye, Barbara!

The End

Reference

"2 CORINTHIANS 13:11 KJV "Finally, brethren, farewell. Be perfect, be of good comfort, be of one mind, live in peace; and the God..." *King James Bible*, https://www.kingjamesbibleonline. org/2-Corinthians-13-11/. Accessed 26 May 2023.

Sister Definition & Meaning. (2023, June 24). Merriam-Webster. Retrieved July 3, 2023, from https://www.merriam-webster. com/dictionary/sister

October 13ᵗʰ Zodiac Sign — Libra Traits, Careers, Mantras & More. (2022, December 28). Popular Vedic Science. Retrieved July 3, 2023, from https://popularvedicscience.com/astrology/october-13-zodiac-sign/

American Cancer Society. (n.d.). *See Cancer Facts & Figures for African American/Black People for Any Year.* American Cancer Society. Retrieved July 3, 2023, from https://www.cancer.org/research/cancer-facts-statistics/cancer-facts-figures-for-african-americans.html

Cancer prevention: 7 tips to reduce your risk. (2022, December 9). Mayo Clinic. Retrieved July 4, 2023, from https://www.mayoclinic. org/healthy-lifestyle/adult-health/in-depth/cancer-prevention/art-20044816

CEI: Helping seniors live at home instead of a nursing home. (2023, June 5). Center for Elders' Independence. Retrieved July 9, 2023, from https://cei.elders.org/about-cei/

The Trustees of the University of Pennsylvania. (2023). Sciatica . Pennmedicine.org. https://www.pennmedicine. org/for-patients-and-visitors/patient-information/ conditions-treated-a-to-z/sciatica

Wang, S. (2021, October 15). *Adele's "Easy On Me" Lyrics Meaning, Explained.* NYLON. Retrieved July 14, 2023, from https://www.nylon.com/entertainment/adeles-easy-on-me-lyrics-meaning-explained

Smith, M.A., M., & Robinson, L. (2023, February 23). *Bereavement: Grieving the Loss of a Loved One.* HelpGuide.org. https://www. helpguide.org/articles/grief/bereavement-grieving-the-deat h-of-a-loved-one.htm

Lansom, A., Romano, K., & O'Sullivan, S. (2020, March 27). *Sisters With Large Age Gaps Talk Childhood Experiences.* Refinery29. Retrieved July 16, 2023, from https://www.refinery29.com/ en-gb/siblings-large-age-gaps

Morrow, A. (2020, March 22). *Getting Through Grief and Letting Go.* Verywell Health. Retrieved July 16, 2023, from https://www. verywellhealth.com/letting-go-of-grief-1132548

Mangan, Doireann. "Akosua - Baby Name Meaning, Origin and Popularity." *The Bump*, 16 May 2023, https://www.thebump. com/b/akosua-baby-name. Accessed 26 May 2023.

Asaaba. (2021, February 2). *Ghana Fashion in 3D.* Accra Archive. Retrieved May 26, 2023, from https://www.accraarchive.com/ blog/i8lii4bbn01flunyo8srdajj7977rn

(PHILIPPIANS 4:13 KJV "I Can Do All Things Through Christ Which Strengtheneth Me." n.d.)

About the Author

Award Winning Author Patricia A. Saunders was born and raised in Connecticut before relocating to the San Francisco Bay Area thirty years ago. After the passing of her mother in 2006, who had Alzheimer's, Patricia decided if she inherited the ugly disease her words would be her legacy. Pursuing her dream of continuing her education, she received her Master's in Management from the University of Phoenix in 2011. In 2012, she let the words flow to the pages and released her first book. Her mantra "Letting the words flow until the pen stops" began. Now releasing her seventh book. Her mantra *"Letting the words flow until the pen stops"* began.

Her work has been featured on a Coast to Coast Book Tour at the Los Angeles Times Festival of Books, Toronto Word On

The Street, Sacramento Black Book Fair, Tucson Book Festival, Miami International Festival of Books, AARP Life@50+ Spring Convention, and The Congressional Black Caucus Foundation Annual Convention. Also, she appeared in *In the Company of a Poet, Women Owned Business Club Magazine*, Alysha Live! Radio Show and Coach Deb Bailey's Secret of Success Talk Radio. She performs locally at spoken word events and Capital Jazz SuperCruise Open Mic with Grammy Award Winner Eric Roberson.

She is a monthly blogger of "Blessed & Curvy," which covers today's hot topics.

She is a certified Motivational Speaker who focuses on women's issues, women empowerment, and grief.

She released her first self-published book, *Through the Fire* (March 2012), which covered emotions from situations, circumstances, and life lessons that have influenced her over her lifetime. On a mission to complete a book a year in the case she inherits the ugly disease she released her second book *Loving Me* (2013), and her third, *Let It Rain* (2014) which is also self-published and covers various topics from love, grief, self-image, self-esteem, bullying, and discovery of self-love. Her fourth book (2016), *This Too Shall Pass,* was released by AuthorHouse Publishing, and readers have given it a five-star rating. *There is Sunshine After The Rain* (2018), a memoir, and *Four Seasons Of Love* (2020). Saunders's seventh book, *"Saying Goodbye,"* is a memoir dedicated to her late sister.

Saunders is a proud member of Delta Sigma Theta Sorority, Inc. She enjoys traveling, spending time with family, and wine tasting in her spare time.

Her books are available at your local book retailers, www.patriciaasaunders.com, www.amazon.com, and www.barnesandnoble.com

You can follow her on social media:
Facebook: @ blessedpoetpat
Instagram:@blessedpoetpat
Blog: www.blessedpoetpat.blogspot.com